As I Remember

A Personal History
For Washington Residents

Introduced by Paul Dorpat

This edition of *As I Remember* by:

_____
Name

_____
Date

Sasquatch Books

INVITATION TO AUTHORS:

The Washington State Archives would like to receive a copy of your personal history. Please send an 8½-by-11-inch photocopy of your *As I Remember* with your name and current address to:

State Archivist
Division of Archives and Records Management
Office of the Secretary of State
P.O. Box 9000
Olympia, WA 98504

The Archives will send you a certificate and the catalog number of your contribution. Unless otherwise noted by the author at the time of submission, individual editions of *As I Remember* shall be considered to be in the public domain and shall be available for publication, in whole or in part, provided proper credit is extended to the author.

Copyright ©1989 by Sasquatch Books
All rights reserved.
ISBN 0-912365-19-6
Printed in the United States of America

This book is printed on acid-free paper.

Cover design by Jane Kathryn Rady
Cover illustration by Lisa Irwin
Interior design by Jini Choi
Editor: Anne Depue
Consultant: Phyllis Harmon, oral historian, *Living History*, Strafford, Vermont
Typeset in Times Roman by Weekly Typography & Graphic Design, Seattle

Sponsored by the 1989 Washington Centennial Commission

Sasquatch Books
1931 Second Avenue
Seattle, Washington 98101
(206) 441-5555

Also by Sasquatch Books with assistance from the 1989 Washington Centennial Commission
  Washingtonians: A Biographical Portrait of the State

INTRODUCTION

All of us who have had some part in the publishing of this book understand that our success will be measured by our fading away as you, the book's real author, materialize. You are the "I" in *As I Remember*. Like the other authors of this book, you are a Washingtonian, whether you were born in the state or arrived here last week. This book is made for you, and the seeds we have planted here will blossom in the colors of your own prose. However, since writers are often reluctant to start writing, we will begin for you.

Once upon a time, Washington State engaged its older residents in one of those Depression-time public works which profoundly helped private lives. It is an oft-noted irony that great depressions can propel a community to greater acts of charity; the "Washington Pioneer Project" assisted the state's first pioneers in leaving for us and their families an important legacy. Begun in 1936, the program was a friendly way to gather oral histories from the state's senior citizens. Ten interviewers hand-recorded over 900 reminiscences statewide. The result was 24.2 cubic feet of correspondences, photographs, memoranda, and oral interviews. Excerpts of the interviews were published in three volumes entitled *Told by the Pioneers*.

In 1936, at the start of this program, the state was three years short of celebrating its Golden Anniversary. Now, in the watch of Washington's centennial, we begin again to encourage citizens to recollect and to produce a revealing portrait of our state. It will be a very different portrait from the one painted by the pioneers, who told of crossing the plains in wagons, fishing in salmon-rich streams, and meeting the hardships and rewards that attended homesteading the wilderness. The pages of this book will no doubt tell of rapid growth and technological change, and the challenges of living in the twentieth century, as well as the personal relationships that have shaped your life.

Today's society often gives personal history a short sheet. Most of us know very little about the generations that preceded ours; indeed, most of us know very little about the past lives of our parents and grandparents. Had your relatives used a book like this one, however, that might be different. You could not only enjoy their reminiscences now—you could also use them in the pages that follow. So you might begin to write this book because your grandparents did not, and because you want to help your children's children to know you and your world a little better.

Perhaps your forebears did write something approximating this book. As part of a community more active in literary pursuits, your grandparents—and theirs—may have kept diaries or journals, or written long and thoughtful letters. Before the telephone made it possible to be in instant communication, friends and family members separated by the Great American Desert, or by a ride across town, nourished one another and their writing by sharing elaborate correspondences. Reviving any literary exercise makes us part of several

The simplicity of the Indian mother's life, although she performed much hard labor, allowed her more time to devote to the care of her children than the average white woman. A great deal of soft moss is used in packing the little baby on its board. This moss takes the place of the linen used in civilized life, and saves much washing.

millennia of reflective culture. So perhaps you should also write this book to be writing.

But to write history you must take time out from making it. While substituting thoughtful reflection for the routines of patter and chatter, you will get to know yourself better. As the title of this book may be read, re-membering is also a process in which you continuously put yourself back together. Although *As I Remember* is not meant to be a daily record written to yourself, you should write this book *for* yourself. You should also write it for your family, friends, and even for your state.

The writing of your personal history may also set you free from the mistakes others are bound to make in remembering your life for you. You may want, then, to write this book for the facts. But accuracy need not limit creativity. "A foolish consistency is the hobgoblin of little minds." Ralph Waldo Emerson's epigram is good advice for writers who worry too much about "getting it straight." Your memories will never be as consistent as your fingerprints; with personal history the truth is always a little crooked. While picking through the yard sale of your past, you will discover that what was has inevitably been influenced by what might and should have been. You will also find that you want to tell a good story, and you may wish to teach a few lessons as well. There is no one correct way to write a personal history. Whatever your approach, let your memories be turned on the wheels of art and analogy as you give shape to your life's time line.

In the foreword to the first volume of *Told by the Pioneers* is a challenge. "The aim of the volume is to preserve in the language of the pioneers or their children the household tales of

3

early days, and to inspire in students the desire to unearth other stories to be preserved in the future." With your help we can once again take up this challenge. As many have noted, a state —or a person—that abandons its past cannot be trusted with its future. Beneath the centennial seal on the copyright page to your book, the Washington State Archives announces that it awaits the addition of your personal history to its collection. This is good news for students of Washington history, for it is the "household tales" of Washingtonians, the stories of "ordinary" as well as "extraordinary" lives, that make Washington history rich and familiar.

The last page of this journal is reserved for your special message to future Washingtonians. What future those who would become the first Washingtonians imagined in the 1850s when they petitioned Congress for their own state north of the great "River of the West" can be gleaned from an attentive reading of any of the three volumes of *Told by the Pioneers*. Becoming "Washingtonians" was the first surprise for these settlers. They wanted to be named after the river. However, the hopes of these "Columbians" were frustrated when Kentucky congressman Richard H. Stanton attached an amendment to the petition dropping the name Columbia and substituting that of Washington. This centennial marks 136 years since the Stanton switch, and all subsequent Washingtonians whose mail has wound up in Washington, D.C., have found amusing the Southerner's explanation that he

*O*ur mail and supplies came in by tri-weekly boats. You know, try to make it the first week, and then make it the next.

4

wished to avoid confusion of the new territory with the old District of Columbia.

After Washington was separated from Oregon in the spring of 1853, its first U.S. marshal, J. Patton Anderson, hurried west to take a census of the new territory. The results of Anderson's impossible task would prove speculative at best. The '53 division enclosed all of Idaho and the western side of Montana, and the marshal did not include any natives in his census, only settlers. He counted 3,965 of them. As one of the 4.5 million Washingtonians now living in this state, it is very unlikely that you are a descendant of one of those first few thousand settlers. Of course, if you are a native American your family's chances of pre-territorial continuity are much better. Whatever the vintage of your Washington heritage, you speak for the state.

Before Gutenberg invented movable type, most books were handcopied by skilled monks working in drafty scriptoriums. The borders of those books were often illuminated, and no two copies were the same. As your writing begins to fill out the shape of these pages, this medieval analogy may occur to you. Your book will also be handwritten and the borders of its pages are illuminated—here with historical photographs and the recollections of other Washingtonians. Every page will be unique.

The recollections were chosen from a number of Evergreen State sources—including the 1936 Washington Pioneer Project. They are intended to serve as suggestive aphorisms or stimulants for your own writing. The photographs, too, are meant to spark your memory. They are revealing records, not only of Washingtonians, but also of the art of photography in this state. We have not limited our selection to photographers who use the word "art" in their calling cards; some of the best of these photographs have been copied from family albums.

The questions we have grouped near the beginning of the book's six sections may be minded or ignored. They are questions we might ask if we were to visit you with a tape recorder. But a book is not a tape recorder. With writing you can make several drafts, compose from an outline, and pause without having to hit a pause button.

Actually, you might first tell your story to a tape recorder—a favorite gadget of writers whose ideas appear at unexpected times and often with such a rush that the hand collapses in an exhausted scribble. Editing a recording will then groom the tape's enthused rambling with the cooler deliberations of the pen. However, we cannot claim that working from drafts, recorded or

There's things I would have liked to ask her I think of now, not then. So many things I would love to know about my family but I don't know. When I was 30 years old, you live alone with them and you don't think of much of what maybe 40, 50, 60 years later is going to be.

written, is necessarily better than going straight to the blank page. Should you begin by plunging in, the hand will either restrain you or you will need to harness it. The general rule with tapes, drafts, and outlines is to use anything that will help you begin, and occasionally use whatever is necessary to slow you down.

The three Rs for doing personal history are Relax, Reflect, and Recollect. The fourth R is wRite. And once you move from the first three toward the fourth, you may need the fifth—Research. The rewards that attend the hide-and-seek of research are so many and so rich that you may find it hard to return to the writing.

Persons who have difficulty discarding the random stuff of life are favored when the time comes to do personal history. A paper trail of programs, menus, doodles, school annuals, love letters, and much more winds through their closets, attics, and garages. More fortunate yet are those who have neatly organized the paper ephemera of their past in scrapbooks and file cabinets. However you or your family have collected your past, some of it has, no doubt, survived to provide clues that might spark a memory long forgotten.

If you have not been an assiduous collector, you may want to research outside sources for details about yourself or your family's past. Most public libraries collect a good selection of regional publications; old newspapers are peculiarly rich records of events that shaped you. Libraries also gather other materials relevant to your life, and the larger ones have history desks with genealogy records, attended by persons skilled in researching both community and personal history.

We were obliged to make a day camp—the wind was blowing a hurricane so that we were unable to build even a sage brush fire. Locking the wheels of the wagons to keep the wind from running them down a chasm, we went thirsty, hungry and dusty to bed.

Other official public records may also be helpful in uncovering some part of your past. The paper morgues of the great bureaucracies contain a wealth of material—county tax assessor records on the history of your family's property; public works department information on your streets and parks. Schools and alumni associations, military services, clubs, banks, title companies, unions, and, for a few Washingtonians, the FBI may also have fragments of your past on file. There is a chance your church has kept the names of those who sang soprano with you in the children's choir and that the hospital will have a record of the wit whose bed was next to yours and who consoled you on the loss of your appendix.

You may wish to begin your research at the back of this book where we have listed a variety of community genealogical societies and historical societies. Besides the library, these two types of organizations can give you a good deal of help in your search. Often community historical societies will have museums attached which will warrant a visit. Like the Washington State Archives, they will be pleased to receive a copy of your history into their own collections.

But, most often, your best source of inspiration and information will be those who have known you intimately: your friends and family. Here again is where a tape recorder can be very helpful. And if your writing features your family, you may persuade another of its members to help with the interviewing.

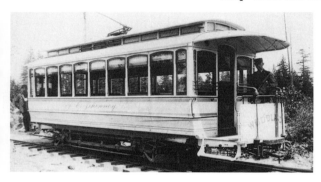

Some books with intentions like this one's abound with questions requiring terse answers in small spaces. As noted above, although we have put a few prompting questions at the beginning of your chapters, you don't have to answer them. The chapters we have chosen are neither over- nor underwrought. We drew three lines across the wheel of life to make six chapters: Beginnings, Growing Up, Homes, Work, Adventures, and Reflections. Like the circle of life itself, these areas inevitably overlap, and they are not intended to be restrictive. For example, if your life's work involved the important task of raising a family and keeping a household going, you may wish to write about it in the Homes rather than the Work chapter. And you may find that you have more memories than there are pages—so we encourage you to have an extra notebook handy.

You do not have to begin at the beginning. You may wish to begin at the Work chapter with a recollection of how you got your first job. If you begin with a recounting of your sudden return from a camping trip in southern Mexico, your first inscriptions would appear near the end of the book, in the Adventures chapter. Or you may wish to begin at the beginning, revealing how you got your name and what you think of it. Finally, if you are too young to

I came West to Washington, as so many Tennesseans were doing. I came by the Union Pacific Railroad to San Francisco and by the Queen of the Pacific to Portland. I was the first on board to get seasick and the last to recover after the boat had crossed the Columbia River bar.

10

have experienced much of what the questions cover, you may wish to use this book to write the history of an older Washingtonian.

Wherever or however you begin, with writing or research, now is the time for you to take control of these pages. Unlike the monks, you will not be copying texts but originating them. Begin with the confidence that you are, and will always be, the genius of yourself.

" *Were these 'Good Old Days' so wonderful? I believe the 'Good Old Days' are only fond memories.* **"**

"**I** remember when I was four or five years old someone asked me what my middle initial stood for. Father said, 'I named him after President Polk. When I named him, the president had taken a strong stand of "54-40 or fight." Polk reversed his attitude on that question and I have been sorry I called my boy after him ever since. Sometimes I have a notion to wring the youngster's neck, I am so disgusted with President Polk.' "

William Polk Gray got his middle name because his father, William Henry Gray, supported James Knox Polk's stance against the British either to make the 54–40 north latitude Oregon's northern border or to fight for it. Later, however, Polk cooled down and agreed to the 1846 compromise that placed the line at the 49th parallel, Washington's present border with Canada. The "54-40 or fight" hotheads, including W.H. Gray, felt betrayed by Polk's diplomacy and their loyalty to the president was severely shaken.

" A prized possession of our boyhood was a jackknife. "

William Gray, Jr. survived his father's disappointment and Anglophobia and lived to become a famous river pilot on the upper Columbia and one of the founders of Pasco. Like most of us, he learned about his beginnings from his parents. You will find that some of your early history is easy to come by—it may have been told to you, or you may have overheard it in conversations. We encourage you to begin this personal history by concentrating on the facts of your family and your origins. You may, like the captain of a ship, wish to begin this log by recording its simplest certainties—where you are now, the date, and your name...all of your names. Once your position has been logged, you can begin to chart the events surrounding your birth. You will probably need to ask yourself and others many questions. Below are a few queries to help you embark on the passage back to your beginnings.

QUESTIONS

When and where were you born? How did you get your name? Have you ever had a nickname? Did you ever want to change your name?

How did your parents meet? When were they married? How long were they married before you were born? Were you adopted, or did you ever think you might have been adopted?

Do you know the names of your great-grandparents? Your great-great-grandparents? Which, if any, of these families immigrated to America? Where did they emigrate from, and why did they leave for America?

When did you or your family move to Washington? Have you ever lived anywhere else? What attracted you or your family to Washington?

Are there any old stories told about your ancestors? Does your family have any particular traditions, and how far back can they be traced? Does your family own any heirlooms or keepsakes, and do you know the story behind them?

What anecdotes reveal best the character of your mother? Your father? What do you know about their childhood(s)? Can you describe your first memories of your grandparents? Did you have a favorite aunt or uncle? A special cousin?

What is your very first memory? What are the favorite family stories about your childhood?

There was a slight sense of disappointment at the change of name, for the word "Oregon" had grown very dear to me as the name of the country wherein lay my "ideal home." But "a rose by any other name would smell as sweet," and I soon grew reconciled to the change. Washington is a name that is suggestive of all that is noble, grand and good.

14

❝ *I went home about once a month, at which time my mother filled my suitcase with cookies, bread, homemade sausage and other edibles.* **❞**

15

We were told that our son was going to be released that afternoon. So again, we drove over to Tacoma and this time they did let my husband and me in. And when we did, here's this little six-year-old kid; he was lying on his side and just crying, but silently, you couldn't hear him. And he said, "Oh, take me back to the camp. They were going to let me die last night." I said, "What are you talking about?" And he said, "Well, the nurse said, 'Let this little Jap die, don't even go near him.'" And to this day he remembers that. He's forty-five years old now, but he still remembers that.

Strange as it seems, it was a common practice in those days for women to be allowed to go to the head of the line, such was the gallantry of the men.

I was born in Washington Territory, three miles south of the present town of Meyers Falls on my father's homestead of 160 acres, June 15, 1852. There were twelve children in the family, six boys and six girls, nine of whom, including myself, were born on this homestead.

19

*O*n Halloween, we put
tack-tack on the window
....and the old man
would get mad and get
up and come out and say
"Rousebadden" and
we'd run.

20

" *I was born in 1847. My mother was an Indian. Our school term was for three months, May, June and July.* **"**

T he people of the settlement were like one large family and a spirit of kindliness and neighborliness pervaded the atmosphere from one end of the island to the other.

*Jeanine
Spencer*

"**I** had to be, but who? Like Alice, I became this enormous girl, these big feet, these other parts, this overwhelming lurid dream. I was bigger than everyone. I was drawn to mirrors to check in. Stampeding through the halls at Lincoln. Swept into the mad pressure of the hive, banging into walls and doors but missing the proms. I was desperately trying to become Elizabeth Taylor...no matter how long I stared in the mirror, or gazed at her picture, I could not become her. Not only that, I was destined for several years of warring with violent pimples and romantic delusions of boys I never talked to...I was constantly confounded by the duality of human nature and the gland system. Art, choir, and plays held me fast to the dream of what might be. If only I could stop eating....I decided that if I was not famous by age 30, I would commit suicide in some dramatic fashion. I knew nothing of the real world."

Jeanine Spencer remembered her teens for "All My Somedays, A Living History Project," a program involving hundreds of Pierce County residents in the process of helping one another recall and record their life stories.

Some of Spencer's teen memories (and her swimsuit snapshot) were included in the exhibit "The Years of Our Teens: Teenagers 1862-1981." Besides the exhibit, the Pierce County Library's writing program also resulted in 120 books of participants' reminiscences, and a play drawn from those memoirs, which Spencer titled *A Loaf of Bread and a Bus Ticket Home.*

The adventurous turns in Jeanine Spencer's growing up began soon after her birth in the hardest years of the Great Depression. Unable to care for her, Jeanine's mother gave her to her

roommate, a retired vaudevillian, who carted the three-year-old off to Tacoma. There Jeanine eventually found a home with an aging aunt and uncle—a home she still lives and writes in.

Growing up in postwar Tacoma, the good-humored Spencer characterizes herself as "somebody who came out of the fifties absolutely prepared for nothing. Nobody talked to you very much in the fifties." So she took her lessons in movies—the jazzy bohemian freedoms of Gene Kelly in *An American in Paris* were especially instructive.

While she had little trouble identifying the typical obsessions of adolescence, many of the older participants in the Living History Project—some of whom Spencer helped with their writing—claimed never to have been teen-agers. Children one day, they were adults the next. Elsie Heritage, writing of her own pre-World War One adolescence, insisted, "I can't remember being a teenager; all I can remember is hard work."

Although most of our growing up seems to take place in our teens, years that seem particularly exhilarating, painful, and filled with frustration, it is a life-long process. However old you are now, here are a few questions which might stimulate a reliving of your past and an intimation of your future.

QUESTIONS What do you remember about growing up with your brothers and sisters? What were some of the games you played as a child? Who were the characters in your neighborhood? What was your most memorable birthday or holiday? What were the rules your parents imposed? How would you describe yourself as a child or teen-ager? Who might have described you differently?

> **❝** *As there was no school available I was taught my 3R's by my mother and my dearly loved grandmother.* **❞**

What did you enjoy most about learning and/or school? Which of all your teachers inspired you the most? What were your favorite and least favorite classes?

Describe some of your best friends from your early years. What was the toughest part about growing up? Who gave you the most help?

What traditions were practiced in your home at holidays and on special occasions? Was there a tooth fairy? Whom did you trick and whom did you treat? Describe a typical weekend in your family. How did you spend your summers?

Who were, and who are, your heroes and heroines? Was there a particular movie star or celebrity whom you envied as a child, teen-ager, adult?

What was your social class as a teen-ager? Were you popular? What were some of the expressions or slang that you used? Review some of the musical, athletic, and entertainment highlights of your youth. What was the first book you read? Did you grow up watching television, or did your children?

Who was your first crush? Do you remember your first kiss? Can you write about it? Did you agree with the sexual attitudes of the time? And now?

When and how did you leave home—was it suddenly or in steps? What did you miss the most? How did marriage—if you are married—change your life? Have you been divorced, or did your parents divorce while you were growing up? How did the experience affect you?

How has the process of growing up continued after childhood? What are some of the crises you have faced?

We had some dreadful soap. It was not like the scented laundry soap of today, but the old barred, sticky rosin soap that was our toilet soap.

25

*T*he sandpile was a treasured fraternity. My brother, Homer, was just two years older than I and for playmates and partners in our activities we had the sons of the prospector, the black-smith, the saloon keeper and the corner groceryman.

26

" *She passed through adolescence in months that took me years. Street knowledge pours into high schools these days. When I was in high school there was only the street...no knowledge.* **"**

*T*erms like "So's yer ol' man" and "keen" and "bee's-knees" didn't roll easily off my tongue. I was a lump.

I met my husband Vic
in July of 1957. I had
went to work at Nalley's
Valley in the onion room
and when I walked in I
seen this nice looking
man with the most beauti-
ful soft blue eyes and full
of tears. I said to myself,
Oh the poor man he
must of just got the news
his mother died! Then it
hit me: onion juice. He
was the head onion
peeler. He was short but
had a very nice build and
big shoulders. . . .

29

We had all kinds of foot races and field events and a ball game on the Third with fireworks and a band concert at night but the Fourth was the big day of days.

What was special about Charlie? Probably nothing, except that he was my first love, the person through whom I learned what excitement is, what strange and moving feelings could course through me at the thought or the nearness of him.

" *Every Fourth of July grandfather made an oak cannon for us bound with iron hoops....We would stuff it full, putting wads of paper and whatever we could find in it, brace it with rocks, and touch a rod to the powder tube, not knowing just where it would shoot. It's a wonder we weren't killed.* **"**

*W*hen we went to school the woods were so dense that after we left the clearing at home we could not see the sky except in two or three places.

*Phoebe
Judson*

"To me it is a source of great satisfaction to see the silent wilderness grown pregnant with human life, and dotted with beautiful homes."

Phoebe Judson was 93 when she published her reminiscences in 1925. Not so long ago, really. With her husband Holden she traveled west on the Oregon Trail in 1853, the year Washington Territory was divided from Oregon. Twenty years old and seven months pregnant when they left Kansas, she lived under roofs which are a revealing sampling of the shelters many a Washington pioneer raised in their "search for an ideal home."

The first, of course, was the home the Judsons brought with them: the wagon. And the second was a cabin built of fir logs and cedar shakes, for their claim at Grand Mound in Thurston County. "We were comfortable all winter without glass in the windows, and when gathered around our fir bark fire in the large clay fireplace, with the children, our cabin was bright and cheerful."

Next, like most other settlers, the Judsons built a bigger cabin, one with squared timbers and dovetailed corners. "We bought glass for the windows, and when the partitions were in we had quite a respectable house, at least one we appreciated more than many a millionaire of these modern times his costly mansion."

The Judsons' search for an ideal home was interrupted in 1855 when they joined thirty other pioneer families in a blockhouse during the Indian War—for sixteen months! The Judson family became pioneers again and moved north to Whatcom County in 1872. There, beside the Nooksack River, they constructed a log house, with a fireplace built with brick brought up the

A typical day at our house started not long after the clock in the dining room struck five. Father would get up and start the kitchen fire at five thirty.

The Danville Cabin Aug. 23/9.

66 *My father built a two story log house of cotton-wood trees, growing along the river. I am sorry to say I tore it down.* 99

river from Bellingham. For Phoebe, "A sense of satisfaction came over me that I have never before experienced in any of my former homes. Surely, this must be the spot for which we had been searching for so many years, where we should build our 'ideal home.' "

And it was. In her time, the wilderness around the Judson cabin became "pregnant with human life, and dotted with beautiful homes" cared for by the citizens of Lynden. And Phoebe Judson became known—and is still remembered—as "The Mother of Lynden." Her husband Holden was the town's first mayor.

But many pioneers expected their own children to hold on to the homes they had built. And so, the pattern of the restless pioneer was often dropped for the security of the established estate.

Your experience may lie somewhere in between. Your first home was probably your parents'. Then you may have begun to practice homemaking in someone else's home or your own. At any rate, you probably share some of Phoebe Judson's desire to search for an ideal home.

Whatever has become of you, your houses, and your homes, there's lots to remember and, as Phoebe Judson reminds us, much to tell.

Here are a few questions you might ask yourself. No doubt you will think of many more.

QUESTIONS

What is your first memory of your family home? Can you draw a sketch and floor plan of it? What was your favorite room in the house? Did you have any pets?

Did the family home have a parlor or room that was only used on special occasions? Did your parents take any special delight in gardening? What were your responsibilities around the house?

What class of neighborhood did you grow up in? Who were your next-door neighbors? Describe the sights and sounds of your neighborhood.

What kind of art was hung on your parents' walls? Describe your dream home. . . .

How many moves have you made? Did you ever live in student housing? Did you iron your own clothes? When did you move into your own home or apartment?

Have you purchased your home? Was it much of a struggle to get it and keep it going? Have you ever built or remodeled your own home? What is the most unusual dwelling you've lived in? Did you or do you have children in your home? How did life at home change as your children were born? If you have children, when did you first leave them and your home in the care of a babysitter? If you have gone through a divorce, how was your home disposed of?

If you are a renter, what sort of landlords have you had? Did you (or would you) help any of your children buy a home? What does having a home mean to you?

M y father built a fine, two-story . . . house with two large fireplaces . . . . He made all his own furniture, some of which was hewn from logs.

35

66 Holiday times we had parties and danced from Christmas until one week after the New Year. We had very good feeds, cakes, game, fish, chicken, roast pigs and puddings. There wasn't much drinking, just a little liquor for the men. We had lovely times. 99

The first Christmas celebration with a tree was held in Mills store. I was nine years old.... There were no Christmas tree ornaments. String pop corn did double duty. Every child had a present and a big bag of candy. My sister and I received a red heart-shaped pin cushion and were speechless with joy.

" *There is nothing that now has the flavor of the food so cooked. Mother could bake the best bread ever made.* **"**

We ate, naturally, mush and milk in the morning. She (my mother) was Scotch. She didn't have much time for fancy cooking. She was a little bit near-sighted and eight kids, you know, and doing the housework and every- thing else—except on Monday the washwoman came.

66 We slept five in a bed. The bed was pushed back to the wall during the day and out into the middle of the room at night. The cabin was one of two rooms. My mother made the quilts real long, so that they could be tucked in around the sleepers. 99

" I had the thrilling experience of cooking a meal for a man at the point of a gun. He acted like a bold, bad man, which we read about, riding up to the door on horseback, knocking on it with his whip. "

I can remember as a little boy sitting up night after night helping my mother with the carding and spinning.... I was nearly grown before I tasted anything made out of white flour.

The applehouse was even more intriguing, having spring water running through it to keep the apples cool.

W O R K

William D.
Vaughn

I baked my bread in a flat kettle, made expressly for the purpose, called a "Dutch oven," by heaping coals on the cover and underneath, replenishing when needed. Bread can be baked very nicely by this method. It was very light and I felt quite proud of my success. When done, I turned it out on the grass to cool, while I attended to my house-work in our wagon home. Hearing the merry laughter of the children, I glanced in that direction, and what was my dismay to see little Annie stand-ing on my precious loaf.

"I worked in Oregon until spring and then, with sixty-eight others, bought a fine brig worth $50,000 for $4000, as sailors could not be had to take vessels away. In the brig we went to Queen Charlotte's island...hunting for gold. We found nothing, and the majority voted to sail for Puget Sound....I now went to work on the Sound getting out piles and square timber. In the spring of '53 I got a team of four yoke of oxen and went to loading vessels for myself, employing six men and getting $40 per day over expenses....In the spring of '54 I built the first log scow on Puget Sound. I carried Colonel Ebey's stock to Whidbey island...I bought into a saw mill, at the same time...on Tulalip bay. Lumber was $20 per 1000 when I bought, and it immediately dropped to $8....The fall in price made me a poor man."

From the day he left home at the age of fifteen, William D. Vaughn worked—as a teamster, a logger, a miner, a shipper, a cattleman, a longshoreman, a road builder, a rancher, a boat builder, a gunsmith, and a hunter. Of all the occupations he worked at, Vaughn was best with a gun. Sometimes he would have to hock it for grub, but more often it relieved him, and those who depended on his aim, from the pangs of hunger and the threat of outlaws or wronged Indians.

Vaughn made his way west in 1851 as a hunter for a wagon train. His reminiscences of his life are so direct and unembellished that the reader is unlikely ever to question the extraordinary record of his attempts to stay alive and out of debt in a wild land.

"After the war I was three months trading in cattle and made $1050, and then I went to logging again. I loaded brigantine with spars for China, making $10 a day. Then I took a government contract, building a military road from the Puyallup river to the White river....I then bought a ranch....Times began to get dull and little to do..."

To get out of debt, William D. Vaughn joined the gold rush to the Canadian Cariboo Mountains. He spent seven strenuous years in the mines, before he decided "to come down."

Vaughn wrote about his life in response to the Old Settler's Contest run by *The Tacoma Ledger* in 1892. The prize was a free trip to the 1893 Columbia Exposition in Chicago and, the newspaper promised, the prize would be awarded "wholly on the merits of the incident described and not at all on the way the story is told." Vaughn didn't win. Perhaps the many pages he packed with the details of his life's labor exhausted the judges. But then, Vaughn probably couldn't have made the trip anyway:

"I am getting old and feeble, and have poor health. I have had the la grippe the last two winters. When I was in the mines I had one shoulder broken..."

Unable to work or move without pain, the indomitable Vaughn puttered with a panacea: a perpetual motion machine.

Although it is unlikely that our several vocations have involved the relentless push of pioneers like Vaughn, his inventor's dream that a machine with perpetual motion might relieve him—and us—from rpms is downright appealing. Here are a few questions on work which you might consider at your leisure.

I worked very hard when I was a child, helping with the housework and all kinds of work on the farm. I worked in the fields; wheat, potatoes, etc.

What was your first job? What was your father's and mother's attitude toward work? What did your parents want you to be when you grew up? What did you want to be?

Did you have prescribed chores around the house? Did you receive an allowance for your work at home? Did you work after school and during summer vacation? Did you have a dream vocation? Did you go to college? Did you take career counseling in school?

Were you expected to get married and leave the work to your husband? Can you describe your experiences of raising a family? What did you feel when your children left home?

Were you ever in the military? Did you enlist or were you drafted? Describe your military experience. Was it everything the recruiter promised? Do you use your military training now?

What is the poorest you have ever been, and how did you get out of poverty? Have you ever lived through a depression, or did your parents tell you stories of the Great Depression? How has your economic situation changed? Did you ever try any wild investments?

What do you consider your greatest professional or domestic achievement? What sort of contributions have you made to your company or profession or family? How much intrinsic pleasure do you take in your work?

What sort of employers have you known? Do you remember your first raise? Were you ever unfairly passed over for a promotion? Are you, or were you, anxious to retire?

What is the hardest you have ever worked? Have you ever done volunteer work? What is your attitude to persons who are out of work? To persons who are on welfare?

Are you creative? Have you ever invented, or dreamed of inventing, something?

*I*n a few years I was in a khaki uniform and joined by comrades in singing "It's a Long, Long Way to Tipperary. . . ."

66I never heard my mother say one word bad about anybody. Only thing she ever said bad was to a minister come into our house. The Presbyterian minister came up to our house and I can hear him right now. I was only a little tiny bugger, and he said to my mother, "Kate, why haven't you been to church? And she said, "Reverend John, why haven't you been up here workin' in my garden, and why haven't you been milkin' these cows, and why haven't you helped me feed these children? And another thing, John, do you think you could give a little more time and maybe help me do the washin' for these eight children of mine, and dad, and Daniel, and grandma? 99

We were to pick three fifteen pound pails of cherries a day for our room and board. Every cherry over that was ours.

*W*ednesday 1st. Gave the men a blowout similar to that which they had on Christmas day which afforded them ample enjoyment. The frost weather continues.

49

I received thirty dollars a month and paid ten dollars a month for my board. I was rich.

> "*Best bait all around was the angle worm. With a tin can for container we could get a supply very handily at the base of the manure piles by the livery barns.*"

Sometimes I had to hurry home after school to get the butter churned before supper. It took fifteen minutes working the plunger up and down in the porcelain churn to bring the cream to butter. At night most of the family activities centered about one oil lamp.

*T*he Hudson's Bay
Company trading post
did quite a big business
when I was a boy. The
store was usually full of
Indians and mixed
bloods. Martin, mink,
muskrat, coyote, bear and
other skins were brought
in, in large quantities and
traded in for merchandise.

*Philemon
Beecher
Van Trump*

*It is Emerson who says,
"We are as much
strangers to nature as we
are aliens from God."*

"I obtained my first grand view of the mountain in August 1867, from one of the prairies southeast of Olympia...Its lofty triple summit towered immeasurably above the picturesque foothills...I then and there vowed, almost with fervency, that I would some day stand upon its glorious summit. If that feat were possible to human effort and endurance."

The object of Philemon Beecher Van Trump's desire was Washington State's great alp of adventure—Mount Rainier. On August 17, 1870, the 31-year-old Van Trump and his companion were, by most accounts, the first to reach the summit of the Mountain. There, exhausted and without blankets, the two huddled beside the steam heat and sulfuric stink escaping from the vents in the summit's smaller crater. It was a life-saving discovery. Freezing on one side and cooking on the other, they turned like rotisseries throughout a sleepless night.

Van Trump had the bravado to advance into any adventure. On this climb, his partner—the son of Washington Territory's first governor, Isaac Stevens—was appropriately named Hazard. Van Trump possessed a wonderful self-confidence that is common among adventurers— especially those who take their risks with nature. And, as his life-long friend Hazard Stevens described him, he was "humorous, generous, and whole-souled."

The generous Van Trump continued to call on the "endurance and human effort" necessary to reach the summit. In 1888, he led the celebrated naturalist, John Muir, up Rainier. They were accompanied by Seattle photographer A.C. Warner, whose records of the expedition include their successful summit. In 1891, Dr. Warren Riley and his deerhound followed Van Trump in

the first ascent of the Mountain from the west side. The doctor's dog was the first canine to reach the top.

Washington State's anatomy—its waterways, coulees, buttes, mountains, and the Mountain —has made outdoor adventures a natural part of most of our lives. Van Trump was fond of promoting the "revivifying ozone of the mountain air at the line of perpetual snow." In prose that sometimes matched the purple mountain's majesty, he wrote, "Few will want to climb to the summit. Hundreds can visit it in search of health, to regain lost appetites, to revive torpid livers, to forget for a time the business, toil and cares of life... He will return with a brighter view of life, and with better hopes of heaven..."

As Van Trump knew, going on adventure need not pose a threat to life and limb. Still, a good excursion includes some playful exploration of the unknown; while not living dangerously, adventurers in travel, love, and ideas need not play it too safe. Below are some bold questions which you may risk answering.

QUESTIONS

Were you encouraged as a child to take physical risks, like doing somersaults from the back fence? Did you excel in any sport? Did you ever win a trip to a neighboring city or island? When did you first explore the limits of your neighborhood?

Did you ever run away from home? Where did you go on your first trip with your family —to visit relatives? What was your first adventure alone? Did your family go on camping trips, and if so how far from home?

Did you ever climb a mountain? Did you ever think of climbing Mt. Rainier? What is your favorite Washington landscape?

Have you ever taken up the study of a foreign land or language or traveled abroad? What faux pas did you commit, or fear committing, while traveling? Did you ever lose anything while traveling? Your health? Are adventures in eating high on your list of risks?

How do you spend your weekends? Do you have any hobbies? Do you play or follow any sports? Is reading a book an adventure for you?

Is there any one event that seems the most exciting thing that ever happened to you? What adventures surprised you, disappointed you? Have you kept in touch with any friends you made while traveling? Were you ever rescued by a complete stranger?

What are the various means of transportation you have used? Did you ever do anything especially risky? Was it also foolhardy? When did you take your first plane trip? If you were asked to fly a mission on the shuttle, would you do it?

Have you ever subscribed to a season of the symphony, opera, or theater? Where does shopping rank in your order of adventure? How do you feel about public speaking or performing before a crowd on any occasion? What place have altruistic adventures, like helping with a food bank or protecting wildlife, had in your life?

Do you consider anyone the model for your adventurous soul? What adventures do you intend to take? Describe the adventure of your wildest dreams. . . .

It was only necessary to go there and watch the run and pick out the one you wanted, because the fish were so thick that they could not get away.

"...as I was a bit of a tomboy I enjoyed climbing trees, playing in the hay loft or at Indians in the woods and working in the plot that had been given me for my very own garden."

> **"** There were many kinds of marbles. The dough baby was not considered much. The "aggies" in many colors and sizes were highly prized. **"**

*T*hey had good horses in those days and riding was a pleasure. The whole family would embark on horses every Sunday morning and go to mass at the mission. After mass everyone would go to Kettle Falls and fish with hook and line, and we used to have gay times there.... According to a French custom, parents arranged the match. I married a man 21 years older when I was 14. I had not seen him until a week before I was engaged to him.

57

I remember a sleighriding party, when the snow was too deep for cars. We started at the end of the line with a sled and team and picked up everyone along the way. We sang as we huddled on the straw bed, covered with warm robes. The air was crisp and tangy. In some places the drifts were so deep it would seem the horses couldn't make it through, but when urged, they would leap and plunge until they cleared the drifts.

" It was the concensus of opinion that it would be impossible to handle her in strong winds. No one was anxious to handle the job. The very difficulty of handling such a Noah's Ark of a boat appealed to me and I applied for the position and was given the job before I could change my mind. "

*M*any of us can
recollect when there was
no radio or television...

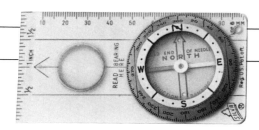

❝ *I wasn't too interested in cooking or being a housewife. Automobile racing was a new thing. I thought being a lady race car driver would be exciting. Barney Oldfield was a hero in my life.* **❞**

I swore I'd never kill another Black Bear after the last one I killed. I happened to shoot this bear at quite a distance off. He was walking along and I shot him a little high and broke his back. He had to stop, of course, and when I went up to him, he acted very much like a human being. I got to be ashamed of myself for killing him. I swore right there I'd never kill another one. I never did.

61

"My husband had joined the army at the age of fourteen, serving as a drummer boy and later as a regular soldier. He had fought in the Civil war. After we were married we used to ride the Kansas plains and shoot buffalo. I was as good a shot as my husband, and could bring down the game as deftly and easily as he, while riding my horse at breakneck speed."

*Ezra
Meeker*

*The Pioneer has no
time to sit in the shadow
of the setting sun looking
backwards. He must ever
be in the vanguard, with
a vision for the future,
surrounded by the beauties
of nature and nurtured
under conditions of mind
and body expansion in-
cident to Pioneer life. I
am sure that we have not
fully appreciated our
privileges.*

"Four years ago to-day I arrived at the ripe age of three score years and ten, sup-posed to be the limit of life. Finding that I possessed more ambition than strength, and that my disposition for a strenuous life was greater than my power of physical endurance, I naturally turned to other fields of work."

What Ezra Meeker turned to was writing, and with Meeker writing meant reflecting. His book *Pioneer Reminiscences on Puget Sound* is one of the best-loved Washington State exam-ples of that popular pioneer genre, not only for the excitement of its many stories, but also for the reflections on a long life whose energy was bounded as much by compassion as by ambition.

In 1852 the 21-year-old Meeker, his wife Eliza, and their six-week-old baby started west on a trek of forced maturation: "I left Indiana a boy and arrived in Oregon a man." After settling briefly at Kalama on the Columbia River, the family moved first to McNeil Island on Puget Sound and then, during the Indian War of 1855–56, to the safety of Fort Steilacoom. It was at the 1857 Steilacoom trial of the Nisqually headman, Leschi, accused of murdering Volunteer Colonel A. B. Moses, that Meeker showed his moral nerve. Refusing to be swayed by postwar hysteria and the settlers' intent on revenge, he and one other member of the jury refused to convict. It required a second trial, this time in Olympia, to send Leschi to the gallows. Years later, in his book subtitled *The Tragedy of Leschi*, Meeker reflected on his protest. He continued to defend the Indian's right to protect his native land and rendered an elaborate reconstruction of the events, including detailed evidence of Leschi's innocence in the death of Moses.

At the conclusion of the war, the Meeker family, like most others on Puget Sound, was down and nearly out. When they took possession in 1862 of a squatter's cabin in the Puyallup Valley, Ezra's cold-weather gear consisted of a blanket with a hole cut in the center for his head. Three years later he planted a handful of hop roots, and from those cuttings the plants, and the man, took off. In a few years Ezra Meeker became known as "The Hop King of the World," and a 17-room mansion (now a Puyallup museum) replaced the squatter's cabin.

Success diluted neither the courage nor integrity of Meeker's inclinations. During the infamous Chinese riots of 1885, Ezra stood before a hostile Tacoma Chamber of Commerce unsuccessfully defending the rights of the Chinese against the citywide clamor to run them out of town. Earlier, in a letter to *The Tacoma Ledger*, he warned those of conscience, ". . . so long as we keep silence, and neither by word or action, say or do aught to counteract the pernicious effects certain to follow in the wake of this agitation, our silence will properly be construed as an endorsement of the cry, 'The Chinese Must Go.' "

Ezra Meeker published his reminiscences in 1905. In 1906, at the age of 75, he drove an ox team back over the Oregon Trail, placing markers and making speeches along the way. In the other Washington, Meeker took his team for a meeting with President Teddy Roosevelt.

When Ezra Meeker died in 1928 at the age of 98, among his items donated to the Washington State Historical Society's Museum in Tacoma was the wagon used in 1906 to retrace the Oregon Trail. Many years later someone thought to look in the wagon's seat-lockers. There they discovered sixteen boxes of Meeker's writings—the records of a life that was not only extraordinarily effective but also consistently reflective.

66 We would go to the movies most of the time to eye the guys more than the movie. 99

What is the first strong sense of self—your self—that you recall? Was there any one person who had a profound effect on the way you thought of yourself and how you looked on life? When you were young were you impressed by any great acts of kindness or generosity? Have any hardships or tragedies awakened you to life's preciousness?

What was the religious atmosphere in your family home? What are some of the philosophies you have ascribed to in your life? Have you had any recurring or memorable dreams that influenced your waking life?

How do your opinions diverge from your parents' beliefs? What have your learned from your children? Will you sometimes take unpopular stands on controversial subjects such as race, human rights, and the military? Do you feel that you always have to be right?

Have art, literature, and other products of the imagination played a part in your sense of what is possible? Do you have a favorite novel? How would you rate your sense of humor? Do your most profound insights come suddenly or usually after long study?

Have you made many mistakes about the character of either new or old acquaintances? Do you feel you have many irrational fears or phobias that do not bother other people? How have you responded to requests for your advice on controversial or touchy subjects?

How have your thoughts and values changed over the years? What values have you tried to instill in your children? Do you have any regrets? Can you look back and see a turning point in your life? What would you do differently? What are some of the best decisions you have made? What do you look back upon with pride or satisfaction?

I was never homesick a day and lived every moment of my life.

65

“ *You and I both do best by taking bold, self-relying courses. I never once failed in my life from the boldness of my course.* ”

I have voted ever since I have had the chance, and now that I can't go to the polls, the polls are brought to me.

The tall shrubs of the red currants, the lovely syringas, plumes of the tassel wood, with the low delicate trilliums, and violets, helped to dispel the gloom of the somber forests. While later in the season our eyes were charmed, and our senses delighted by the delicate coloring and delightful fragrances of the wild rose.

It was one of Washington's loveliest October days, brightened by the snow-capped peaks of the mountains glistening in the morning sunshine; and the gorgeous hues of the maple foliage on the low lands, with the background of the ever green fir and cedar, presenting a landscape that could hardly be surpassed for grandeur, or one more refreshing to the souls of the weary emigrants.

*O*ne of the soldiers asked me if I would dance a waltz. I consented, so he went to the fiddlers and persuaded them to play a waltz tune, and we started dancing. After waltzing twice around the hall we noticed no one else was dancing. I was satisfied that this soldier and I danced the first waltz ever danced in Spokane.

69

I think the young ladies were as proud of their new flannel dresses as the girls of today are of their fine store clothes.

66 Compared with life today, we went through many hardships and had few of the wonderful advantages offered young people now. Yet I believe that in spite of those hardships, or maybe because of them, we were better fitted for life than young people of today, for this reason: hardships are stepping stones to people of ambition. 99

While the pioneer was often tired in body, or troubled in soul, he was seldom the victim of frayed nerves, or of that physical or mental languor called ennui.

You are part of Washington State's history. Pass on your story to present and future Washingtonians through the state's special centennial collection. See copyright page for details.

F A M I L Y T R E E

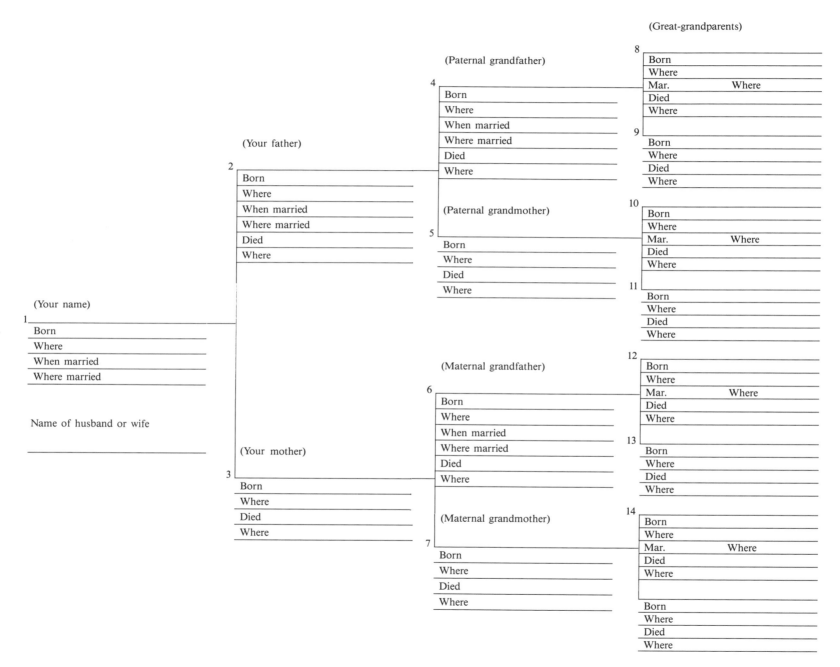

(Great-grandparents)

(Paternal grandfather)

8
Born
Where
Mar.   Where
Died
Where

4
Born
Where
When married
Where married
Died
Where

(Your father)

9
Born
Where
Died
Where

2
Born
Where
When married
Where married
Died
Where

(Paternal grandmother)

10
Born
Where
Mar.   Where
Died
Where

5
Born
Where
Died
Where

11
Born
Where
Died
Where

(Your name)

1
Born
Where
When married
Where married

Name of husband or wife

12
Born
Where
Mar.   Where
Died
Where

(Maternal grandfather)

6
Born
Where
When married
Where married
Died
Where

13
Born
Where
Died
Where

(Your mother)

3
Born
Where
Died
Where

(Maternal grandmother)

14
Born
Where
Mar.   Where
Died
Where

7
Born
Where
Died
Where

Born
Where
Died
Where

74

A P P E N D I X

HISTORICAL SOCIETIES

Adam East Museum
5th and Balsam
Moses Lake, WA 98837

Adams County Historical Society Museum
Phillips Building
Lind, WA 99341

Anderson Island Historical Society
Johnson Farm
Anderson Island, WA 98303

Asotin County Historical Society
P.O. Box 367
Asotin, WA 99402

Association of King County Historical
   Organizations
P.O. Box 3257
Seattle, WA 98114

Bainbridge Island Historical Society
P.O. Box 10003
Winslow, WA 98110

Benton County Museum & Historical Society
P.O. Box 591
Prosser, WA 99350

Black Diamond Historical Society
P.O. Box 232
Black Diamond, WA 98010

Black Heritage Society of Washington State
P.O. Box 22565
Seattle, WA 98122

Chelan County Historical Society
P.O. Box 22
Cashmere, WA 98815

Clallam County Historical Society
P.O. Box 1024
Port Angeles, WA 98362

Clark County Historical Museum
P.O. Box 1834
Vancouver, WA 98660

Cle Elum Historical Society
Mail: 202 Reed St
Cle Elum, WA 98922

Cowlitz County Historical Society
405 Allen St
Kelso, WA 98626

Du Pont Historical Museum
207 Brandywine Ave
Du Pont, WA 98327

Duvall Historical and Old Stuff Society
P.O. Box 342
Duvall, WA 98019

East Benton County Historical Society
P.O. Box 6710
Kennewick, WA 99336

Eastern Lewis County Historical Society
P.O. Box 777
Morton, WA 98356

Eastern Washington State Historical Society
W 2316 1st Ave
Spokane, WA 99204

Eatonville Historical Society
R.R. 2 Box 444
Eatonville, WA 98328

Edmonds–South Snohomish County
   Historical Society
P.O. Box 52
Edmonds, WA 98020

Ethnic Heritage Council of the Pacific
   Northwest
1107 NE 45th St, Suite 315-A
Seattle, WA 98105

Ezra Meeker Historical Society Inc.
P.O. Box 103
Puyallup, WA 98371

Ferry County Historical Society
P.O. Box 497
Republic, WA 99166

Ft. George Wright Historical Museum
P.O. Box 7496
Spokane, WA 99207

Fort Lewis Military Museum
Bldg 4320, Main St
Fort Lewis, WA 98433

Fort Nisqually Museum
Point Defiance Park
Tacoma, WA 98407

Fort Vancouver Historical Society
P.O. Box 1834
Vancouver, WA 98668

Fort Walla Walla Museum Complex
P.O. Box 1616
Walla Walla, WA 99362

Fox Island Historical Society
1017 9th Ave
Fox Island, WA 98333

Franklin County Historical Society
P.O. Box 1033
Pasco, WA 99301

Granite Falls Historical Society
P.O. Box 135
Granite Falls, WA 98252

Greater Des Moines–Zenith Historical Society
P.O. Box 98033
Des Moines, WA 98188

Greater Woodinville Historical Society
P.O. Box 495
Woodinville, WA 98926

Hanford Science Center
P.O. Box 800
Richland, WA 99352

Historical Office/Washington State
   National Guard
Camp Murray
Tacoma, WA 98430

Historical Society of Seattle & King County
2161 E Hamlin St
Seattle, WA 98112

Ilwaco Heritage Foundation
P.O. Box 153
Ilwaco, WA 98624

Index Historical Society
P.O. Box 107
Index, WA 98256

Island County Historical Society
P.O. Box 305
Coupeville, WA 98239

Issaquah Historical Society
P.O. Box 695
Issaquah, WA 98027

Jefferson County Historical Society
210 Madison St
Port Townsend, WA 98368

King County Office of Historic Preservation
618 2nd Ave, 805 Alaska Bldg
Seattle, WA 98104

Kitsap County Historical Society
3343 NW Byron St
Silverdale, WA 98383

Kittitas County Museum
P.O. Box 265
Ellensburg, WA 98926

Lake Chelan Historical Society
P.O. Box 1948
Chelan, WA 98816

Lewis County Historical Society and Museum
599 NW Front St
Chehalis, WA 98532

Longmire Museum
General Delivery
Longmire, WA 98397

Lopez Island Historical Society and Museum
P.O. Box 163
Lopez Island, WA 98261

Makah Cultural and Research Center
P.O. Box 95
Neah Bay, WA 98357

Maple Valley Historical Society and Museum
P.O. Box 123
Maple Valley, WA 98038

Marymoor Museum
P.O. Box 162
Redmond, WA 98073

Mason County Historical Society
P.O. Box 843
Belfair, WA 98528

Museum of History and Industry
2700 24th Ave E
Seattle, WA 98112

Museum of Native American Cultures
P.O. Box 3044
Spokane, WA 99220

National Archives–Seattle Branch
6125 Sand Point Way NE
Seattle, WA 98115

Newcastle Historical Society
14553 SE 55th St
Bellevue, WA 98006

Okanogan County Historical Society
P.O. Box 1129
Okanogan, WA 98840

Oregon Province Archives of the Society
 of Jesus
Crosby Library
Gonzaga University
Spokane, WA 99258

Othello Community Museum
P.O. Box 121
Othello, WA 99344

Pacific County Historical Society and
 Museum Foundation
P.O. Box P
South Bend, WA 98586

Peninsula Historical Society
P.O. Box 744
Gig Harbor, WA 98335

Polson Park and Museum Historical Society
P.O. Box 432
Hoquiam, WA 98550

Puget Sound Maritime Historical Society
2161 E Hamlin St
Seattle, WA 98112

Renton Historical Society and Museum
235 Mill Ave S
Renton, WA 98055

Roslyn Historical Museum Society
Roslyn, WA 98941

Salmon Beach Historical Committee
P.O. Box 7002
Tacoma, WA 98407

San Juan Historical Society
P.O. Box 441
Friday Harbor, WA 98250

Shaw Island Library & Historical Society
Shaw Island, WA 98286

Shoreline Historical Museum Inc.
P.O. Box 7171
Seattle, WA 98133

Skagit County Historical Society
P.O. Box 818
La Conner, WA 98257

Skamania County Historical Society
P.O. Box 396
Stevenson, WA 98648

Snohomish County Museum & Historical
 Association
2602 Rainier St
Everett, WA 98201

Snohomish Historical Society
P.O. Box 174
Snohomish, WA 98290

Snoqualmie Valley Historical Society
P.O. Box 179
North Bend, WA 98045

South Thurston County Historical Society
P.O. Box 339
Tenino, WA 98589

Spokane Valley Historical Society
E 10303 Sprague Ave
Spokane, WA 99206

State Capitol Historical Association
211 W 21st Ave
Olympia, WA 98501

Steilacoom Historical Museum Association
P.O. Box 16
Steilacoom, WA 98388

Stevens County Historical Society
P.O. Box 25
Colville, WA 99114

Sumner Historical Society
P.O. Box 517
Sumner, WA 98390

Sunnyside Museum & Historical Association
P.O. Box 782
Sunnyside, WA 98944

Suquamish Tribal Cultural Center and
 Museum
P.O. Box 498
Suquamish, WA 98392

Toppenish Museum
1 S Elm
Toppenish, WA 98948

Tumwater Historical Association
602 Des Chutes Way
Tumwater, WA 98501

Vashon Maury Island Heritage Association
P.O. Box 723
Vashon, WA 98070

Waitsburg Historical Society
P.O. Box 277
Waitsburg, WA 99361

Walla Walla Valley Pioneer and Historical
 Society
P.O. Box 1616
Walla Walla, WA 99362

Washington State Archives Regional Branch
3 Sunset Activity Center
1809 S 140th St
Seattle, WA 98168

Washington State Historical Society
315 N Stadium Way
Tacoma, WA 98403

Washington Trust for Historic Preservation
111 W 21st Ave
Olympia, WA 98501

Whatcom County Historical Society
P.O. Box 2116
Bellingham, WA 98227

White River Valley Historical Society
918 H St SE
Auburn, WA 98002

Whitman County Historical Society
P.O. Box 67
Colfax, WA 99111

Yakima Nation Museum
P.O. Box 151
Toppenish, WA 98948

Yakima Valley Museum & Historical
  Association
2105 Tieton Dr
Yakima, WA 98902

GENEALOGICAL SOURCES

Genealogy Collection
Seattle Public Library
1000 Fourth Avenue
Seattle, WA 98104

Seattle Genealogical Society
PO Box 549
Seattle, WA 98111

National Archives—Seattle Branch
6125 Sand Point Way NE
Seattle, WA 98115

Whitman County Genealogical Society
PO Box 393
Pullman, WA 99163

BIBLIOGRAPHY

All My Somedays. (Catalog for "The Years of Our Teens," a traveling exhibit cosponsored by Pierce County and Tacoma Public Library.) Tacoma: 1981.

Bennett, Robert A. *A Small World of Our Own: Authentic Pioneer Stories of the Pacific Northwest from the Old Settlers Contest of 1892.* Walla Walla: Pioneer Press Books, 1985.

Brewster, David, and David M. Buerge. *Washingtonians: A Biographical Portrait of the State.* Seattle: Sasquatch Books, 1988.

Denny, Arthur A. *Pioneer Days on Puget Sound.* Edited by Alice Harriman. Seattle: The Alice Harriman Co., 1908.

Gibson, Lillian, ed. *My God Techer I Can Read: An Anecdotal Account of Former Days in Washington's Schools.* Washington State Retired Teachers Association, 1976.

Jones, Roy Franklin. *Boundary Town: Early Days in a Northwest Boundary Town.* Vancouver, Wash.: Fleet Printing Co., 1958.

Judson, Phoebe Goodell. *A Pioneer's Search for an Ideal Home: A Book of Personal Memoirs.* Lincoln and London: University of Nebraska Press, 1984 (reprinted from the original 1925 edition).

Miles, Charles, and O.B. Sperlin, eds. *Building a State: Washington 1889-1939.* Tacoma: Washington State Historical Society, 1940.

Owens, John. *White River Valley History.* Auburn, Wash.: White River Valley Historical Society, 1982.

Rinehart, Ward. *Covello: A Pioneer Remembers.* College Place, Wash.: Color Press, 1975.

Scheuerman, Richard D. and Clifford E. Trafzer. *The Volga Germans: Pioneers of the Northwest.* Moscow: University of Idaho Press, 1980.

Sheller, Roscoe. *Blowsand.* Yakima: Franklin Press, 1966.

Washington Pioneer Project, *Told by the Pioneers: Tales of Frontier Life as Told by Those Who Remember the Days of the Territory and Early Statehood of Washington.* Vol. 1-3. W.P.A. Sponsored Federal Project: 1938.

Whiting, Jeanne L. *Yarrow a Place: An Historical Commentary on Lives and Times During the Early Development of Yarrow Point.* Yarrow Point, Wash.: 1976.

QUOTE SOURCES

Page 2, Judson, *A Pioneer's Search for an Ideal Home,* 96.

Page 3, Judson, *A Pioneer's Search,* 225.

Page 4, Washington Pioneer Project, *Told by the Pioneers,* vol. 3, 143.

Page 5, *Told by the Pioneers,* vol. 3, 60-61.

Page 7, Iola Bazinet (interview), from the Skagit County Historical Museum, RIII-86, 21.

Page 8, Judson, *A Pioneer's Search,* 69.

Page 9, *Told by the Pioneers,* vol. 3, 62.

Page 10, *Told by the Pioneers,* vol. 2, 200.

Page 11, Owens, *Vignettes,* 3.

Page 13, Jones, *Boundary Town,* 35.

Page 14, Judson, *A Pioneer's Search,* 85.

Page 15, Gibson, *My God Techer,* 157.

Page 16, Brewster, *Washingtonians,* 372.

Page 17, *Told by the Pioneers,* vol. 3, 139.

Page 18, Bill Bessner, Skipper of Guemes Island Ferry (interview), RIII 81 from the Skagit County Historical Museum, 12.

Page 19, *Told by the Pioneers,* vol. 1, 144.

Page 20, Arthur Laframboise (interview, 1973), 18.

Page 21, *All My Somedays,* 11.

Page 22, *above, Told by the Pioneers,* vol. 1, 89.

Page, 22, *below, Told by the Pioneers,* vol. 2, 120.

Page 24, *Told by the Pioneers,* vol. 1, 155.

Page 25, *above,* Whiting, *Yarrow,* 25.

Page 25, *below, Told by the Pioneers,* vol. 1, 175.

Page 26, Jones, *Boundary Town,* 26.

Page 27, *All My Somedays,* 26.

Page 28, *All My Somedays,* 28.

Page 29, *All My Somedays,* 7.

Page 30, *above,* Frank Wachter (interview), *Skamania County Heritage,* vol. 7, no. 2, Sept. 1978, 7.

Page 30, Jones, *Boundary Town,* 267.

Page 31, *All My Somedays,* 38.

Page 32, *above, Told by the Pioneers,* vol. 3, 10.

Page 32, *below, Told by the Pioneers,* vol. 1, 172.

Page 33, Jones, *Boundary Town,* 13.

Page 34, *Told by the Pioneers,* vol. 3, 171.

Page 35, *above, Told by the Pioneers,* vol. 3, 61.

Page 35, *below, Told by the Pioneers,* vol. 1, 146.

Page 36, *above, Told by the Pioneers,* vol. 1, 145.

Page 36, *below, Told by the Pioneers,* vol. 3, 54.

Page 37, *Told by the Pioneers,* vol. 3, 168.

Page 38, Laframboise, 43.

Page 39, *Told by the Pioneers,* vol. 3, 157.

Page 40, *Told by the Pioneers,* vol. 3, 12.

Page 41, *Told by the Pioneers,* vol. 1, 90.

Page 42, Whiting, *Yarrow,* 19.

Page 43, Judson, *A Pioneer's Search,* 36-37.

Page 44, *Told by the Pioneers,* vol. 1, 144.

Page 46, Jones, *Boundary Town,* 291.

Page 47, Asa "Ace" Jones (interview), reprinted with permission of the Renton Historical Society

Page 48, *All My Somedays*, 8.

Page 49, *Told by the Pioneers*, vol. 1, 28.

Page 50, *Told by the Pioneers*, vol. 3, 193.

Page 51, *above*, Jones, *Boundary Town*, 33.

Page 51, *below*, Jones, *Boundary Town*, 15.

Page 52, *Told by the Pioneers*, vol. 1, 87.

Page 53, Judson, *A Pioneer's Search*, 22.

Page 54, Judson, *A Pioneer's Search*, 305.

Page 55, *Told by the Pioneers*, vol. 1, 90.

Page 56, Whiting, *Yarrow*, 15-16.

Page 57, *above*, Owens, *Vignettes*, 11.

Page 57, *below*, *Told by the Pioneers*, vol. 1, 190.

Page 58, Gibson, *My God Techer*, 158.

Page 59, *Told by the Pioneers*, vol. 1, 100.

Page 60, Owens, *Vignettes*, 5.

Page 61, *above*, *All My Somedays*, 10.

Page 61, *below*, Byron Kibler (interview, 1970), 4.

Page 62, *Told by the Pioneers*, vol. 3, 116.

Page 63, *Told by the Pioneers*, vol. 2, 58.

Page 64, *All My Somedays*, 13.

Page 65, *Told by the Pioneers*, vol. 3, 49.

Page 66, *above*, Brewster, *Washingtonians*, 83.

Page 66, *below*, *Told by the Pioneers*, vol. 3, 21.

Page 67, Judson, *A Pioneer's Search*, 99.

Page 68, Judson, *A Pioneer's Search*, 81.

Page 69, *Told by the Pioneers*, vol. 2, 188.

Page 70, *Told by the Pioneers*, vol. 1, 106.

Page 71, *Told by the Pioneers*, vol. 3, 64.

Page 72, Miles, *Building a State*, 93.

PHOTO CREDITS

Page 1, Museum of History and Industry, Seattle

Page 2, Special Collections Division, University of Washington Libraries, Photo: James Lee, neg. 20016

Page 3, Courtesy of Paul Dorpat

Page 4, Courtesy of Paul Dorpat

Page 9, Museum of History and Industry, Seattle

Page 10, Special Collections Division, UW Libraries, neg. UW 4924

Page 11, Museum of History and Industry, Seattle

Page 13, Historical Society of Seattle and King County

Page 15, Courtesy of Paul Dorpat

Page 16, Special Collections Division, UW Libraries, Photo: Howard Clifford, neg. UW 9685

Page 17, Museum of History and Industry, Seattle

Page 18, Special Collections Division, UW Libraries, Photo: A.C. Warner, neg. UW 9683

Page 19, Museum of History and Industry, Seattle

Page 20, Wing Luke Asian Museum, Seattle

Page 22, Museum of History and Industry, Seattle

Page 23, Courtesy of Jeanine Spencer

Page 24, Courtesy of Paul Dorpat

Page 25, Courtesy of Paul Dorpat

Page 26, Special Collections Division, UW Libraries, neg. UW 4792

Page 27, *below*, Special Collections Division, UW Libraries, Photo: L.G. Linkletter, neg. 9686

Page 28, Courtesy of Paul Dorpat

Page 29, Courtesy of Paul Dorpat

Page 30, Museum of History and Industry, Seattle

Page 31, Courtesy of Paul Dorpat

Page 32, *above*, Courtesy of Paul Dorpat

Page 32, *below*, Special Collections Division, UW Libraries, neg. UW 955

Page 33, Lynden Pioneer Museum, Lynden

Page 34, Courtesy of Paul Dorpat

Page 35, Courtesy of Paul Dorpat

Page 36, Special Collections Division, UW Libraries, Photo: James Lee, neg. 21004

Page 37, Courtesy of Paul Dorpat

Page 38, Special Collections Division, UW Libraries, Photo: James Lee, neg. 20035

Page 39, Courtesy of Paul Dorpat

Page 40, Museum of History and Industry, Seattle

Page 41, Courtesy of Paul Dorpat

Page 42, Museum of History and Industry, Seattle

Page 43, Washington State Historical Society, Tacoma

Page 44, Courtesy of Nick Gunderson

Page 45, Courtesy of Paul Dorpat

Page 46, Special Collections Division, UW Libraries, neg. UW 1530

Page 47, Museum of History and Industry, Seattle

Page 48, Courtesy of Paul Dorpat

Page 49, Courtesy of Paul Dorpat

Page 50, Special Collections Division, UW Libraries, Photo: James Lee, neg. 3145

Page 51, *left*, Courtesy of Paul Dorpat

Page 51, *right*, Special Collections Division, UW Libraries, Photo: John Cobb, UW neg. 9681

Page 52, Museum of History and Industry, Seattle

Page 53, Washington State Historical Society, Tacoma

Page 54, Special Collections Division, UW Libraries, Photo: A.C. Warner, neg. 579

Page 55, *above*, Museum of History and Industry, Seattle

Page 56, *below*, Museum of History and Industry, Seattle

Page 57, Courtesy of Paul Dorpat

Page 58, Courtesy of Jane Rady

Page 59, Courtesy of Paul Dorpat

Page 60, Special Collections Division, UW Libraries, Photo: James Lee, neg. 20056

Page 61, Courtesy of Paul Dorpat

Page 62, Courtesy of Paul Dorpat

Page 63, Courtesy of Paul Dorpat

Page 64, Courtesy of Paul Dorpat

Page 65, Courtesy of Paul Dorpat

Page 66, Museum of History and Industry, Seattle

Page 68, Museum of History and Industry, Seattle

Page 69, Courtesy of Paul Dorpat

Page 70, Museum of History and Industry, Seattle

Page 71, Courtesy of Nick Gunderson

Page 72, Museum of History and Industry, Seattle

Page 73, Museum of History and Industry, Seattle

Object photos by Kim Zumwalt